MW01136135

The Craft & Culture
of Artisan Schnaps

Kirk Ross

Printed in the United States of America.

ISBN 978-0-9910436-2-0

whitemulepress.com
cheers@whitemulepress.com

PO Box 577
Hayward, CA 94541

Für die Familie Warter
Herzlichen Dank für den schönen
Nachmittag beim Brennenunterricht.

For the Warter Family
Thank you for the wonderful
afternoon of distilling lessons.

Das Trinken lernt der Mensch zuerst
Und später erst das Essen
Drum soll er auch aus Dankbarkeit
Das Trinken nicht vergessen!

— Old German drinking proverb

At first, a person learns to drink
Only later learns to eat
So out of deepest gratitude
The drinking should repeat

Contents

~ INTRODUCTION ~

What This Book is Really About

This is not really a book about drinking. In fact, it is not really about alcohol either. The truth is, it really is a book about a particular approach to living.

A few years ago, I had the privilege of spending some time in central Austria at a farmhouse outside of a little village on the border between Salzburg and Styria. Next to the farmhouse stood a small restaurant, which, by the grace of all things beautiful, had its own little Schnaps distillery. The owner, a true distilling artisan, made small batches of Schnaps, which he sold to local hikers who passed his little restaurant on their way up the trails into the mountains.

One late afternoon after a long day of hiking, I sat at a picnic outside the farmhouse with a group of family and friends. The owner brought out a little tabletop still he had, and he spent the next hour making Schnaps right in front of us while he taught us about the process. Then, with the sun setting behind us, and pale sunlight fading from the top of the Alps in front of us, we passed the glass around. I thought to myself, *This guy has got some things figured out. He's his own boss. He lives in the mountains with his family. And he sits outside his farmhouse teaching people how to enjoy some homemade Schnaps while the sun sets.* That is not just a drink. That is a way of life.

I think of that afternoon every now and then when I take a sip of Schnaps. In fact, I thought about it so often that I decided to learn more about how it is made. That inspiration led directly to this book. It goes without saying that, since then, most of the Schnaps I have had, I have drunk in much more mundane environments. But the feeling I had that evening, when the drink in my hand was the perfect distillation of a terrific day, is a feeling I always try to hold on to when I enjoy my next glass of Schnaps.

First, a couple of important points on terminology. This book is about Schnaps—not schnapps. Schnapps is an American drink that is generally pretty low-quality stuff. It is basically stiff vodka that has had some fruit steeping in it for a few weeks. It might be all right for certain parties or as a flavoring agent, but it is not usually meant to be savored. You can usually find it on the bottom shelf at your local liquor store.

Austrian artisan Schnaps is something altogether different. It is a high-quality alcohol distilled directly from fermented fruit. The process has two basic stages. First, ripe, high-quality fruit is fermented to turn its sugar content into alcohol. The resulting slurry is called mash. After the mash has been fermented, it is distilled to separate the alcohol and the fruit flavors and aroma from the remaining fruit matter. The resulting distillate is Schnaps.

Some linguistic purists might point out that there are actually a couple of different words in German for the type of drink we are talking about here. It might be called Edelbrand or Obstbrand or a couple of other things. In fact, a few types of Schnaps are so popular that they have their own name, like Kirschwasser.

Those linguistic purists are absolutely right. However, it is equally true that "Schnaps" is the typical generic word for this type of distilled fruit drink, so that is what we are going to go with.

A final note on terminology goes to the question of culture. Certain distilling aficionados might point out that drinks very similar to the Schnaps described in this book are made in plenty of other places around the world. In France, it might be called *eau-de-vie*. In Bulgaria, it might be called *slivovitz*. And in Greece, they might call it *grappa*. Those aficionados are also correct.

However, the stuff in the glass is only part of the craft of distilling. The other part is the cultural package in which a drink is wrapped. When a distiller talks about *eau-de-vie*, he is (or should be) talking as much about the French culture that produced it as he is about the drink. The same is true of Bulgaria and *slivovitz*, or Greece and *grappa*.

So the Schnaps in this book includes the drinking culture it came from, namely the Austrian Alps. You cannot talk about Scottish whisky without at least mentioning kilts and claymores. And you cannot talk about vodka without trying to say something with a Russian accent. In the same way, you cannot talk about Schnaps without giving a nod to brass bands and girls in dirndls. So that is what we will do.

This book will introduce you to the craft and culture of making and drinking Austrian Schnaps. Chapter 1 begins the book with a brief introduction to the history of distilling and how it made its way to the Alps, where it produced Schnaps. Chapters 2, 3 and 4 dig into the details of how the stuff is made. Chapter 2 gives an overview of the process, including the hard science. Chapter 3 is all about the mash, including some basic recipes. And Chapter 4 is about the actual distilling, including a primer on how stills are made and how they work.

Chapter 5 is a recognition that actually operating a still is a pretty tall order in most parts of the world, particularly given legal realities in many places. So in this chapter I provide an alternative means of making Schnaps without a still of your own. Finally, Chapter 6 shares a few of the more colorful ways Austrians integrate Schnaps into their way of life.

The book closes with three appendices which I hope you find helpful and/or interesting. Appendix A tries to get most of the bad news out of the way in one place. It describes the legal environment for distilling in the US and in the three countries with a strong Schnaps culture: Germany, Austria, and Switzerland.

Appendix B is a German-English glossary of some common Schnaps-related words. Appendix C finishes the book with a list of resources you might want to look into if you are interested in learning more about Schnaps or craft distilling more generally. This is a wonderful time to be a part of the craft distilling movement in the US, so definitely take a look.

Now let's get to it.

~ CHAPTER ONE ~

A Brief History of Schnaps

Somewhere back in the mists of pre-history, some guy in a cave looked at a pot full of old, wet grain or fruit. He saw that it was frothing at the top, and it probably smelled kind of bad. And then of all things, he decided to taste it. I've always wanted to ask that guy exactly what he was thinking. But lucky for us, he did. And thus, the art of making and drinking alcohol entered human history.

Archeology has shown that ancient Sumerians were drinking beer in about 4000 BC. And a thousand years later, Egyptians were drinking sorghum beer and almost thirty varieties of wine. So brewing has been around pretty much forever.

But distilling is a different story. The art of taking a fermented drink and extracting and concentrating the alcohol in it through a process of heating and subsequent cooling did not develop until thousands of years later. I have read competing accounts of where distilling was first discovered. Some sources argue that it first arose in the West. Others argue that it first arose somewhere in the East. Since our focus here is Austrian Schnaps, most decidedly in the West, that is the story I will stick with.

The Western history of distilling starts with Aristotle (talk about a serious pedigree!) around 350 BC. And it even had to do with drinking (although it happened to be water). In his Meteorology, Aristotle argued that all liquids (speaking particularly of wine) when evaporated and re-condensed, actually turn into water. He had no concept of separating out different liquids at different boiling points. He thought boiling actually transformed a liquid into water.

It was all part of his argument about the four basic elements—earth, air, fire, water. So he had the science wrong. But this primitive concept of distilling was useful enough to help ancient sailors who would boil seawater and catch the evaporating steam on pot lids and bundles of cotton. The steam condensed back into fresh water, which the sailors could drink. They did not correctly understand how it worked, but they had freshwater to drink. So it was better than nothing. Aristotle's basic idea was the going theory for the next several hundred years, and his views were repeated by other big names like Pliny the Elder and Dioscorides in the first century AD or so.

The first time we read about something that actually resembles our modern concept of distilling is in Egypt in the third century AD. A couple of hundred years prior to that, two women alchemists named Cleopatra (not *that* Cleopatra) and Mary (not *that* Mary) had written a technical distilling treatise, which we no longer have. Lucky for us though, the third-century historian Zosimus described their primitive alembic still for us in his own work. And in a wonderful little historical twist, Zosimus added to his written description by inserting a drawing of their still into the margins of a Greek-language copy of the biblical Gospel of St. Mark.

The apparatus is primitive and simple. But all the essential pieces are there.

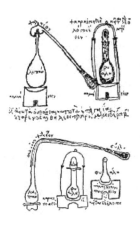

Zosimus' drawing of an alembic still

At the beginning of the seventh century AD, Egypt was an integral part of the Byzantine Empire. By the end of that century, the new Muslim Empire had conquered and annexed the country. Roundabout that time, the Greek-speaking Egyptians passed their knowledge of distilling on to their new, Arabic-speaking masters.

There is some suggestion that the Arabs had known something of distilling prior to conquering Egypt, but it is unclear. What is not at all unclear is that the Arabs enthusiastically embraced this technology for their own alchemical pursuits. The specifics of what they did with distillation is a little outside the scope of our story here, but there is one particular Arab contribution to our topic which really needs to be included.

That critical contribution is the very word "alcohol." The distillates the Arabs made were often used for cosmetic purposes when mixed with other ingredients, and they referred to the resulting products as "al-co-hue," which means something like "finely-ground beauty powder for eye make-up." Kind of a lot to pack into seven letters.

But in any event, the Arab Empire included a motley mix of

tribes in the western end of North Africa, who were collectively known as the Moors. In 711 AD, the Moors invaded and conquered most of the Iberian Peninsula (modern-day Spain and Portugal), and when they did, they brought the Arab knowledge of distilling with them. And that is how Europe was first introduced to distilling.

For the next seven hundred years or so, distilling was strictly to be found in monasteries and other centers of study. This made sense, since the Moors, who had taught it to the Europeans, had presented it as an alchemical process for medicine and research, not for recreational drinking. The European academics who dabbled in it saw it almost exclusively in those terms—chemistry, not gastronomy.

Some of the Middle Ages' biggest names got involved in early distilling, including Albertus Magnus (1193-1280) and Raymundus Lullus (1232-1315). A famous alchemist and doctor named Arnaud de Villeneuve (1235-1311) even thought that the vapors from distillation would provide him with the key to the legendary Philosopher's Stone.

In another unexpected turn of history, a serious outbreak of the plague between 1347 and 1350 was the primary driver behind a major expansion of distilling beyond the monastic walls. Certain distillates were considered helpful against the plague, and as more people got sick, they got more anxious to be able to make the medicine themselves, since it was faster and cheaper than waiting for a doctor to come by.

As a by-product of taking copious amounts of this "medicine," more than a few people began to realize that there might actually be a recreational element in all of this since they ended up tipsy every time they tried to fight off the plague.

So the fifteenth century saw the spread of distilling through the western European countryside. It probably started in parts of France, where people thought distillates could give them longer lives—hence the name *eau-de-vie* which means "water of life." But for our purposes, it also spread through the alpine regions of central Europe, where different regions put their own stamp on the resulting products.

Some of the first popular books we have about distilling were written by a man in Strasbourg named Hieronymus Brunschwig (1450-1513). His *Big Book of Distilling* had over 600 pages and included long lists of recipes for people to try. Obviously, it had not taken long for people to get into hobby distilling.

And our final historical note comes from a very famous Swiss German, whom history knows as Paracelsus (1493-1541). Paracelsus made major waves in almost every field of endeavor he attempted (mostly medicine and theology), but for our purposes, he is best known for one thing. He was the person who gave the final, modern form to the old Arabic word we use for this whole shebang. He coined the word "alcohol." Thank you, Herr Paracelsus.

So this was pretty much the lay of the distilling land for the next several hundred years. But it is really important to remember that one of the major limitations on distilling at this time was the profoundly primitive knowledge of fermentation.

Until the science of yeast was basically invented in the twentieth century, creating a fermented mash of fruit was pretty much a matter of luck. A farmer would put his barrels of old fruit out in the barn and wait for the bubbling to start. After the bubbling stopped, he would distill whatever he had. The quality of the distillate depended to a very great degree on the quality of the resulting mash. And that quality was an iffy thing. There would be plenty of batches which a farmer would just have to throw away.

So for many years, fermenting in the German and Austrian countryside was a good way to do something with fruit that would otherwise just rot. But it was not a guaranteed thing. Some years it might be great, depending on the quality of the mash (among other things). But it might just as easily taste like vinegar. There was a lot of luck involved.

We now know that the primary issue causing the trouble was the indeterminate identity of the yeasts involved in the fermentation. Various strains of yeast float all around us in the air all the time. Some of those yeasts, when added to sugar, produce drinkable alcohol. Those are the ones we like. Other yeasts, in the presence of the same sugars, produce substances which are sometimes undrinkable, and sometimes poisonous. These are obviously the ones to avoid. So when an Austrian farmer put his fruit in the barn to ferment, the specific yeasts that just happened to land on his mash determined the quality and usability of the resulting mash. This was the secret ingredient which no one knew.

However, despite these microbiological limitations, Schnaps still acquired a very important place in local cultural life, particularly (for present purposes) in rural parts of Austria.

This state of affairs began to change in the 1970s and 80s. Science had finally figured what had been up with the yeast for all those centuries, and we could finally regulate fermentation to create consistently good mashes. This obviously led to much better Schnaps. In the last few decades, Schnaps has gone from a matter of chance to a matter of craftsmanship.

And craftsmanship is the theme of the next several chapters.

~ CHAPTER TWO ~

The Big Picture and the Science

Making Schnaps, like just about any other liquor, consists of two basic steps. First, some organic material (usually a food product) with a reasonably high water content and a sufficiently high sugar content is fermented to produce alcohol. Then the resulting product, called a "mash," is distilled in order to remove the resulting alcohol and make it more concentrated.

Chapters 3 and 4 give plenty of specifics on those two steps for the aspiring distiller who just wants to know how to make this nectar. This chapter, though, digs into the science of exactly what is going on in both of these processes. I fully admit that this chapter will get sort of technical, and I happen to love getting into the weeds of this sort of stuff. If this is not the sort of stuff that interests you, feel free to skip to the next chapter. But if you ever hope to become one of the lucky people making distilled drinks for a living, you are probably going to want to know how nature makes all of this possible.

To a scientist, an "alcohol" is any molecule which consists of an oxygen-hydrogen group attached to some other hydrocarbon group. The particular hydrocarbon group is generally what determines the exact type of alcohol in any particular substance, e.g. ethyl alcohol, methyl alcohol, butyl alcohol, etc.

When we, as laymen, speak of alcohol, we are generally referring to drinking alcohol. The drinkable variety is called ethyl alcohol or ethanol. This is the molecule we are trying to create when we make Schnaps, or beer or wine or whiskey, etc. Ethyl alcohol consists of one oxygen-hydrogen group (OH) and one ethyl-group. An ethyl-group consists of a particular arrangement of two carbon atoms and five hydrogen atoms. So our target chemical substance, ethyl alcohol, is chemically designated as CH_3-CH_2-OH.

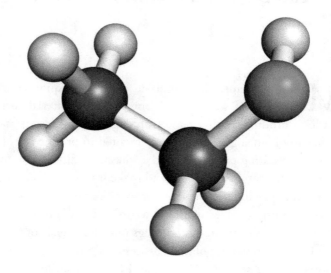

One molecule of ethyl alcohol

FERMENTATION

I bet the question you're asking right now is, *who cares?* Good question. The answer lies in the process of fermentation. Ethyl alcohol does not, as they say, grow on trees. In anything greater than trace amounts, ethanol must be intentionally produced. And we produce it by letting nature do the work for us—with yeast. This is what fermentation does.

Generically speaking, yeast refers to a huge collection of unicellular organisms which live all around us, not to mention *on* us. These thousands of types of yeasts live by eating sugar molecules, which exist everywhere in nature. When they do, they produce various types of alcohols (per the scientific definition), plus carbon dioxide. Some produce methyl alcohol, some produce butyl alcohol, etc. Most of those products are not drinkable. Some of them are poisonous. The trick for the distiller is to find the yeast that produces the specific type of alcohol we want, namely ethyl alcohol.

Luckily, that determination was definitively made in the nineteenth century. For the countless centuries before that, brewers and distillers had to simply leave their mashes in the open air and hope that the right yeast just happened to land in their containers. If they were lucky, they got a good mash and a good drink. If they were not lucky, they got vinegar, or possibly something that made you blind. Luck of the draw.

So living in the 21st century definitely has some advantages for the distilling community. The particular yeast that produces ethanol when it metabolizes sugar is called *Saccharomyces cerevisiae*. Certain strains of this species are better for alcohol production than others, but this is the yeast that has been the central element in fermentation for thousands of years (even when we did not realize it).

That is even where the name of the yeast came from. The word *Cerevisiae* is actually Latin for "of beer." So this is the yeast "of beer." Evidently, even scientists like a drink now and then. That is also why you can usually find it on store shelves, labeled as brewer's yeast or baker's yeast. For the sake of ease, going forward I will just refer to our old friend, *Saccharomyces cerevisiae*, as yeast, since it is the only one that concerns us here. If I ever mean yeast in a more general way, I will make sure to point it out.

So as already mentioned, yeast lives by eating sugar. For purposes of making Schnaps, we can focus on the sugar generally found in fruit, since that will be our base. The common sugar in fruit is known as fructose. Its chemical structure is $C_6H_{12}O_6$.

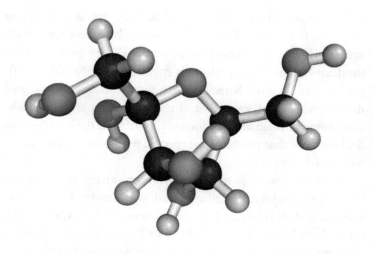

One molecule of frustose

Note that the elements in fructose, namely carbon (gray), hydrogen (white) and oxygen (red), are the same ones as in ethanol. They are just put together in a different way. So we have all the chemical pieces we need. We just need to rearrange them.

That is precisely what yeast does. When it metabolizes, or eats the sugar, it separates various clusters of the various elements and splits fructose molecules into two new types of molecules, namely ethanol and carbon dioxide. In the process, one fructose molecule is broken into two ethanol molecules and two carbon dioxide molecules, plus a little heat generated by the reaction.

And voila! We have our drinking alcohol.

$$C_6H_{12}O_6 \quad \cdots\rightarrow \quad 2\,CH_3\text{-}CH_2\text{-}OH \;+\; 2CO_2 + \text{heat}$$

Fructose   *Yeast*   *Ethanol*   *Carbon Dioxide*

The carbon dioxide that is produced is what comes out in the bubbles and foam in any fermenting process. And the heat produced by the chemical reaction is why mash tends to get warm. The part of the process left in the bucket is the ethanol, which is exactly what we want.

As an important sidebar, fermentation also produces several additional substances which end up in the mash. These include things like glycerin, acetaldehyde, and other alcohols like fusel oils and methanol. The concentration of these substances often depends on the quality of the mash's ingredients and a certain amount of good fortune. To the extent necessary, we will deal with these other byproducts when we discuss distillation.

So at the end of the fermentation process, we have a mash which is full of leftover fruit material soaking in a mixture of ethanol, water and a few other odds and ends. The question then becomes, how do we separate the ethanol and the fruit flavor from all that other stuff, particularly the excess water? The answer to that question is distillation.

DISTILLATION

At its most basic, distillation is built on the fact that water and ethanol have different boiling points. The goal is to boil off more of the ethanol (and collect it elsewhere) while leaving behind more of the water.

At one standard atmosphere of air pressure, i.e. sea-level, water boils at 100°C (212°F). So if a pot of plain water is put on the stove to boil, the water will heat up until it reaches 100°C (212°F). Then it will begin to boil, but the water will not get any hotter. Only after all the water has boiled away will the temperature of the pot itself begin to rise. The water will never heat beyond 100°C (212°F) because that is the temperature at which it changes to steam, at which point it obviously boils off.

The same would be true of a pot full of pure ethanol on the stove, but at a temperature of 78.5°C (173°F), which is ethanol's boiling point. At that temperature, ethanol turns to steam and boils off.

The difference between these two boiling points is the key to distillation. A blend of water and ethanol has a boiling point that is somewhere between 100°C (212°F) and 78.5°C (173°F).

The more water in the mix, the closer the boiling point is to 100°C (212°F), and the more ethanol in the mix, the closer the boiling point moves toward 78.5°C (173°F). In other words, the specific boiling point of the water/ethanol blend is determined by the alcoholic content of the mixture.

When the water/ethanol blend, i.e. the mash, is heated to boiling, the steam which rises from it has a higher ethanol content than the original mash. The steam contains more of the liquid with the lower boiling point, i.e. ethanol, than the liquid with the higher boiling point, i.e. water. This increased concentration of alcohol is precisely what we are trying to accomplish.

At the same time, the fluid remaining in the mash has a steadily increasing proportion of water, since the steam is taking more ethanol than water. Consequently, the boiling point of the mash increases over the course of a distillation run.

% WATER / % ETHANOL	BOILING POINT
0 / 100	78.3°C
10 / 90	78.5°C
20 / 80	79.35°C
30 / 70	80.20°C
40 / 60	81.0°C
50 / 50	81.90°C
60 / 40	83.1°C
80 / 20	87.15°C
90 / 10	91.45°C
100 / 0	100°C

It is important to note that the steam is definitely not just pure ethanol. Given the realities of physics, the vapor includes some substantial share of water, and critically, some of the aroma and taste of the original fruit. This is what gives Schnaps its flavor. But the steam certainly has a much higher ethanol content than the mash, so we are moving in the right direction.

By the way, as a scientific matter, there is a limit to the alcohol concentration you can achieve through distillation. Even if you run the same distillate through your still multiple times, you will never be able to produce 100% ethanol. In fact, the very best you can do is 96% alcohol. This is called the azeotropic point. It is the concentration at which the steam in the still will have the same alcohol concentration as the remaining mash or liquid in the pot. Science beyond simple distilling is necessary at that point to remove the final drops of water.

Luckily, you will almost certainly never need to address this issue if Schnaps is your goal. A typical Schnaps has an alcohol concentration of about 41-43%, so even if your distillate comes out above that concentration, you will likely dilute it down to drinkable strength. And azeotropic alcohol does not have any flavor or aroma anyway, so don't bother.

The final trick is to capture your newly concentrated alcoholic steam and turn it back into something we can drink. To make sure we can do this, the mash is heated in an enclosed container which has some sort of cooling tower on top of it. The vapor cools on its way up the tower, and at the top it is guided into a tube where the steam re-condenses back into a liquid before it pours out into some sort of receptacle.[1] This final product is the stuff we drink – with a certain amount of relish, I might add.

---

1   By the way, this is a very simplistic, but essentially complete, description of every still you will ever see. Read Chapter 4 for the details.

~ CHAPTER THREE ~

Mash and the Fermentation Process

This chapter describes all the steps you will need in order to make a really good Schnaps mash. The first step is deciding exactly what kind of Schnaps you want to make. In other words, what organic material do you plan to ferment into mash?

Fruit is the most typical base for a good Schnaps. Some of the most common fruits for mashing include these:

Apples　Pears　Peaches　Plums
Cherries　Raspberries

But there are also plenty of other options. A lot of other fruits work equally well like kiwi fruit, pineapple, or other berries. In theory, you can make Schnaps from just about any organic material that has sufficiently high sugar and water contents. In fact, I've tasted Schnaps made from a large variety of unusual sources, like Hay Schnaps or Pine Cone Schnaps. And there are plenty of great surprises waiting to be discovered out there.

However, sometimes you get exactly the Schnaps you expect. What I mean is, Hay Schnaps tends to taste exactly like, well—hay. And I don't mean that in a good way. So to be clear, I am a big fan of experimentation, which is the lifeblood of artisan distilling. But it is also true that some foods just work better for distilling, and taste better.

But the organic base is the first of many individual choices every distiller gets to make in order to create his or her own unique flavor. For this book, I will primarily focus on Schnaps made from various types of fruit.

Selecting Your Fruit

The mash is perhaps the most critical step in making good Schnaps. It is simply not possible to make good Schnaps from inferior mash. No amount of fancy distillation work will save you from bad-tasting mash. So this step is vitally important.

You have a couple of options for acquiring your fruit. Most distillers, whether commercial or hobby, get their fruit from the store. This is certainly the easiest way to get the necessary stock of fruit, and it is most likely to be perfectly sufficient for making some really good Schnaps.

If you plan on buying your fruit, your goal should be to buy fruit that is right at the peak of ripeness. And, to the extent you can, you should try to minimize the time lag between when the fruit was picked and when it ended up in the store. And you should try to find fruit that has a minimum of bruises and other damage.

The other approach for obtaining your fruit is to go out and pick it yourself. This is definitely more work-intensive, but many a purist will argue that it will result in a better Schnaps, i.e. better flavor and aroma. At the very least, it certainly gives you greater control over the condition of your fruit.

If you are willing to go to the effort of harvesting your own fruit, then there are a couple of additional tips which will help you get the greatest advantage from that effort.

As with store-bought fruit, you should aim to pick your fruit when it is at the peak of ripeness, not after. One of the great advantages of picking is that it basically eliminates the lag between harvesting and mashing, which helps maximize the sugar content of the fruit.

Another little detail to help increase the sugar content is to try to harvest your fruit after a couple of days of sunny weather. The sun draws the sap and other fluids to the ends of tree and bush branches which is where the fruit is. So the fruit is slightly sweeter.

Try not to pick fruit that is growing near a road. Fruit along roads is likely to have some level of contamination from exhaust fumes and other debris. You do not want that stuff in your mash if you can help it. It can only hurt the flavor (who wants Schnaps with a diesel finish!?).

Finally, do your best to mash your fruit on the same day you pick it. As soon as it has been harvested, fruit begins to chemically decompose. To put it simply, fruit rots as it is decomposed by various bacteria and fungi. And these various bacteria and fungi are precisely the sort of microbes that can seriously mess up a good mash.

The sooner you mash your fruit and get it sealed in a fermenter, the better job you will do avoiding any unwanted microbiology. If, despite your best efforts, you cannot mash on the same day as the harvest, a good Plan B is to freeze your fruit as soon as you pick it. This seriously slows down the decomposition process and keeps the microbes to a minimum. But remember, as soon as you pull the fruit out of the freezer and it begins to thaw, that decomposition process starts right back up.

Whichever method you choose for getting your fruit—buying it or picking it—the key is using fruit that is at the height of its ripeness. This will maximize the aroma and the flavor. For most fruits, this means that it is just starting to feel a little soft, but not at all mushy.

Preparing Your Fruit

So now you have your fruit. Next, you need to get it ready to be mashed. First, the fruit must be clean. Any little microorganisms on the fruit have the potential to screw up the fermentation, so do your best to get rid of them with a thorough washing.

While you are washing the fruit, remove any leaves, stems or rotten sections you may have missed earlier. The leaves and stems are probably pretty obvious, but removing the rotting sections is just as important.

Some people have probably heard the older view that rotting fruit actually makes better mash because it is sweeter than ripe fruit. This view is where we get the name "brandy peaches," which is an older term for peaches which are too rotten to sell. The idea was that they were too rotten to eat, but perfect for making distilled drinks like brandy.

But this older perspective has been proven wrong. It is possible that there is a slightly higher sugar content in partially rotting fruit than in ripe fruit. In theory, this could result in a mash with a marginally higher alcohol content. However, the pathogens that are introduced to the mash from rotting fruit will do much more damage to your ultimate product than any small increase in sugar could possibly justify.

HARVESTING TIPS

• Pick after sunny weather

• Mash (or freeze) the same day you pick

• Avoid fruit near a road

WASHING EXCEPTIONS

Avoid anything more than a cursory washing of fragile bases like flower petals or soft berries. A firm wash will flush away a lot of the juices, which is where much of the aroma and flavor are.

So the best answer is to use fruit that is right at its peak of ripeness, just before it would otherwise start to rot. This maximizes the sugar (and the flavor and aroma) while avoiding those nasty microbes.

Preparing Your Mash

Once you have selected and prepared your fruit of choice, the next step is to prepare the mash. With just a few caveats, this step is really straightforward. Mash the fruit. That is really it—except for the caveats.

There is a wide range of commercial mashing equipment available for distillers who produce a significant amount of Schnaps. However, for hobby or small distillers, there is probably no reason to spend much money on this process. It is much too simple for that.

For soft fruits like berries or bananas, this is a pretty simple step, especially if the fruit is properly ripe. You will simply mash up the fruit with your hands or feet. For somewhat stiffer fruits like apples or pineapple, start by dicing up the fruit as small as you reasonably can with a knife or a food processor.

Now put your fruit in some large container and squish it up. The container can be anything from a large kitchen bowl to something as creative as a small plastic swimming pool like kids use in the backyard. The size of the container just depends on how much mash you're making.

The most important caveat is to make sure that your container is clean (are you seeing a theme here?). Any germs will just pollute your mash. This also means removing as much of the soap as you possibly can after you have cleaned it. Soapy flavors are not what you are looking for.

You may also need to add a little water to your mash, depending on the type of fruit you are using. Some fruits like berries or watermelon have a high enough water content that you do not need to add more. But other fruits, like apples or maybe pears, might need some extra fluid. The goal is to achieve a mash that is sufficiently fluid to allow the yeast to work all through the mash.

Bear in mind that the more water you add, the more diluted the final mash will be (which may mean extra distilling), so you want to minimize the amount of water you add. However, it is equally true that you need to add *enough* water to make the mash work. Practice will help you find that right balance between no more water than necessary *and* no less water than necessary. In any event, water should never comprise more than about one-third of the volume of the mash (and that is really pushing it).

Mashing the fruit does not have to be a very sophisticated process. Like stated above, it can be done in a kitchen with a knife or a food processor. But it can just as easily be done with a pair of good rubber boots (as long as they are clean). Just get the fruit mashed. No matter what method you use, the fruit needs to end up as a slurry.

Another caveat to bear in mind concerns fruits which have pits, like peaches or apricots. In some cases, the pits should be removed from the mash altogether. In other cases, a few should be left in, because they add to the flavor. When in doubt, leaving them in the mash is probably the best way to start.

However, there is one critical issue to remember. The pits *must not* be damaged. That means they must not be broken or cracked. A broken or cracked pit can release cyanide into your mash. This then passes into the distillate. It then passes into your mouth when you drink it. Obviously, that's not good. Fortunately, as long as the pits remain undamaged, there is nothing to worry about. But you might want to remove the pits from the fruit while you squish it up to avoid damaging them. Then you can add them back in, if you want to include them for flavoring.

I know I am beginning to sound like a broken record, but I will add once more—as your fruit is being mashed, it is important to keep the process as hygienic as possible. Whatever new microbes get mashed up with the fruit will end up inside the fermenter. If there are enough unexpected guests in there, the fermentation may not work right, and the mash can be ruined.

Once the fruit is worked to a good pulp, pour it into the container you will use for the fermentation.

Acid and the pH-Value

Before you can begin fermenting, you need to check the pH-value of your mash. Simply put, pH is a measure of the amount of acid in a liquid. More technically, the term pH, *pondus hydrogenii*, means the weight of the hydrogen ions in the liquid solution.

The pH is most typically measured by inserting a short chemically-prepared strip of paper into the mash. The paper turns a certain color, based on the acid level. Then you compare the color of the paper to a simple color palette which tells you the pH-value associated with each color. Everything you need comes in a small, inexpensive kit which you can get at just about any beer or winemaking store.

Yeast can only thrive when the pH-value of the mash is between about 3.0 - 3.3 or so. So check the pH with your kit. If your mash is already in the right range, then you do not need to do anything.

If the pH-value is too high, the mash is not acidic enough for the yeast. This is pretty common. To address the problem, add sufficient acid to lower the pH-value to the correct range. Again, you can get this acid at a winemaking supply shop.

If the pH-value is too low, this means the mash is too acidic for the yeast. This very rarely happens, except in the case where the distiller accidentally added too much acid when the pH was too high. Oops. The solution here is to add a little calcium carbonate until you reach the correct pH.

PH-VALUE	ADD
Too high (over 3.3)	Acid
Too low (under 3.0)	Calcium Carbonate

Extra Sugar

Another possible ingredient to add is a somewhat larger topic—sugar. And by that, I mean plain-old, white table sugar. First, let me say that this ingredient is entirely optional. The sugar in whatever fruit you are using will typically be perfectly sufficient to make a good mash and a good Schnaps.

However, it is also true that the addition of extra sugar *may* make that Schnaps better. As we know, sugar is the root ingredient in the production of ethanol. The sugar in fruit is called fructose. The sugar in your kitchen cupboard is a combination of fructose and its close cousin, glucose. For our purposes, table sugar reacts to yeast in the same way as plain fructose does.

Yeast eats the sugar, and ethanol is the result. So the amount of ethanol that can be produced from a mash is directly tied to the amount of sugar in it. When the yeast has eaten all the sugar, the fermenting process is over, and the mash has all the ethanol it will ever have.

So simple math suggests that adding more sugar will lead to more ethanol. In the abstract, this is true. Adding sugar will produce a mash with a higher ethanol content, which means it will need less distilling to achieve the right drinkable concentration.

However, there is an important caveat. Adding sugar usually means needing to use specialized yeast. In a wonderful little twist of scientific irony, if the alcohol content of a mash gets too high, typical *cerevisiae* yeast cannot survive. So if you add extra sugar to your typical mash, the alcohol content will rise and eventually kill your yeast before all the sugar has been metabolized. Your mash will have a bunch of sugar left in it after fermentation. You could still go ahead and distill it, but the result will be really sweet. And, maybe more importantly, all that sugar is potential ethanol that just got wasted.

If you choose to add sugar (and doing so is not typically necessary), you will need to track down special yeast. These specialty yeasts usually have names like "Super Yeast" or "Turbo Yeast." Just ask for the high-alcohol-content yeast.

Preparing the Yeast

The final piece of the puzzle is the yeast, which will do all the important work. Most yeast comes in its dry form, so you will need to re-hydrate it. The specific directions for activating the yeast will be on the package, but in general, it should be stirred into a bucket half full of water and half full of liquid from the mash. The temperature of the fluid in the bucket should be warm, around 35°C (95°F) or so. The amount of liquid needed will depend on the size mash you are making (keeping in mind that the water for the yeast will constitute part of the total water content of the mash).

And you will probably want to add yeast nutrients. These are certain vitamins and minerals that help the yeast thrive, so they can only be a helpful addition. This process of preparing and activating the yeast is called "pitching" the yeast. Once the yeast has been pitched, it must be used within about fifteen minutes or it will die. So pitch it right when you plan to start fermentation.

Putting It All Together

Now it is time to put the whole package together. The mash should already be in your fermenting container. The container should be a bucket or carboy made of food-grade glass or plastic. Cheap plastic will bleed chemicals into your mash, so avoid them.

Now add the water/yeast mixture to the mash, and stir it in well. The entire mash should not fill more than about three-fourths of the container. Otherwise, the foam of the fermentation may explode the container. Not good.

Left— airlock; right— fermenter with airlock

The fermenting container must be sealed with a lid which includes an airlock. And both pieces of that last sentence are important. First, the fermenter must be sealed air-tight. This will keep out unwanted germs and other bacteria. Second, there must be an airlock.

The airlock is a clever device that is partially filled with water. The airlock allows the carbon dioxide from the fermentation to escape by bubbling through the water while also preventing any foreign microorganisms from getting into the mash.

The fermentation container should be placed in a quiet spot out of bright, direct light, and the ambient temperature should remain between about 15°C (60°C) and 18°C (65°F).

At first, the fermentation should cause some pretty serious bubbling through the airlock. There is plenty of yeast and there is plenty of sugar for it to eat, so there should be quite a party going on in the carboy (or other container). Over the course of the fermentation, this process will slow down as the sugar gets consumed.

Every few days, you should pop open the container and give the mash a good stir. I know what you are thinking—won't this allow all those bad bacteria to get into the mash? Good question. Just having the container open for a few minutes a couple of different times is generally not enough exposure to be a problem. And it is necessary that you get into the mash and break up any solids which may have formed in the mash. Stirring will also get the yeast in better contact with more of the fructose. So it is worth the potential (minimal) contamination.

Another issue to look for when you pop open the fermenter is to check and see if the mash itself is starting to gel or set, making it difficult to stir. This can happen as the yeast works through the mash and starts metabolizing the sugar. The solution to this potential problem is to add an enzyme called pectinase.

Interestingly, yeast itself produces a small amount of pectinase as a by-product of fermentation. And this amount of pectinase sometimes suffices to keep the mash sufficiently fluid. But in many cases, the amount of pectinase produced by the yeast is not enough to prevent the mash from setting. Extra pectinase will prevent this problem. In fact, you may want to just plan ahead and add some extra pectinase at the beginning of the mash. It does no harm to the mash, and it may save you some trouble later.

The fermentation process is completed exactly at that point where there is no sugar left for the yeast to metabolize. It has all been converted to ethanol and CO_2. There are a couple of ways to know when you have reached that point. The first, and most obvious, is that there are no more bubbles coming through the airlock. Confirm this diagnosis by stirring the mash one more time. If no bubbles are stirred up when you do so, then fermentation is probably complete.

For the gearheads out there, the most scientific way to confirm the end of fermentation is with a vinometer. A vinometer allows you to check the alcohol content of your mash. If you check the alcohol content every time you stir the mash, you will note a point where the alcohol content stops increasing. When the alcohol content has flat-lined, fermentation has finished.

Bear in mind that a lack of bubbles might also be connected to a problem with the fermentation rather than its completion. Sometimes, a fermentation stops before all the sugar is metabolized, a problem referred to as a "stuck" fermentation. This can be caused by several things. For example, if the ambient temperature of the fermenting room or space is too low, this can kill the yeast. Or if there are insufficient nutrients in the mash, the yeast may not survive.

SUMMARY

FRUIT
• Ripe, clean fruit with the stems, seeds and rotten sections removed
• Mash to a pulp

WATER
• Add enough to make the mash fluid
• Never more than one-third of the total volume

PH-VALUE
• Between 3.0 and 3.3

PECTINASE
• Add to prevent mash from setting

SUGAR
• Optional, but can be used to increase the alcohol content of a mash

YEAST
• Regular brewer's yeast unless sugar has been added
• With extra sugar, use specialty yeast

FERMENTATION
• Sealed container with an airlock
• Between 15°C and 18°C
• Check and stir every few days

The surest way to make sure that your fermentation is finished rather than stuck is to use the method for measuring the mash's alcohol concentration just described. If the yeast has died in the middle of the process, the alcohol content will be on an upward trajectory before it suddenly stops. In a normal fermentation, the alcohol content rises quickly at first but then tapers off in a measured, gradual way until it flat-lines when fermentation has ended.

Some Specifics

As has been mentioned before, good Schnaps can be made with just about any kind of fruit, not to mention quite a few other sources of Schnaps like flower petals or pine cones. But the list below includes some specific pointers for some basic categories of the most commonly-used fruits.

Berry Schnaps

Berries can produce some very good Schnaps. However, they can be a little labor-intensive.

Given their low sugar content and high water content, it takes a lot of berries to produce a sufficient amount of mash for a useful distillation run.

It was pointed out above, that the ideal situation is to mash fruit on the same day it is picked. For berries, this is even more important since they do not tend to store well. If mashing on the same day is not feasible, then definitely try to freeze them.

You will probably not need to add much (or any) pectinase since berries already contain a high water content and will typically produce a sufficiently fluid mash.

A berry mash should be distilled very soon after fermentation. Otherwise, it may lose its aroma and taste relatively quickly.

A berry mash needs to be brought to a distillation boil even more slowly than usual (see the information on distilling in the upcoming chapters).

Berries are often a very good option for the "Beginner"s Schnaps" described in Chapter 5.

Strawberries: Note that there is a big difference between domestic strawberries and wild strawberries. Domestic berries will be difficult to use for Schnaps, since they have less flavor and more water than their wild cousins. Wild berries have more flavor, but they are smaller, so it takes even more of them to make a mash.

Other common examples: raspberries and blackberries

Seeded-fruit Schnaps

Fruits with seeds have a couple of advantages for the hobby distiller over berries. First, given the higher sugar content and lower water content, it typically does not take quite as much fruit to produce an equivalent amount of mash. Second, there is not quite the same time crunch for seeded-fruit as for berries. Depending on the particular fruit and the condition it is in, it is possible (though perhaps not preferred) to store the fruit for some short period of time.

In the process of mashing the fruit, try not to damage the seeds.

Given their natural density, these fruits will almost certainly need the addition of pectinase and yeast nutrients.

In almost every case, be sure to leave the skins on when mashing since this is where a lot of the flavor is.

Common examples: Apples and pears (one of the most common Schnaps).

Pitted-fruit Schnaps

The biggest issue with these types of fruit is the pit itself. As discussed above, it is important not to damage the pits during mashing. However, it is usually equally important to include some of the pits in the mash since part of the flavor comes from the shells of the pits.

This type of fruit gives the best flavor when it is mashed and distilled directly after being picked. And it is best picked after the fruit has ripened in the sun for a few days.

Depending on the fruit, you will probably need to add pectinase and yeast nutrients.

In almost every case, be sure to leave the skins on when mashing since this is where a lot of the flavor is.

Cherries: Cherry Schnaps is almost its own separate category on most store shelves. It is known as Kirschwasser, a name you may even see on a bottle in the US.

Other common examples: Plums, apricots (another one of the most common Schnaps), nectarines and peaches.

~ CHAPTER FOUR ~

Distilling your Schnaps

Now we get to the fun part. This is the part where you take that bucket full of left-over fruit and water and, with the right application of really cool science and careful technique, artfully draw out the special combination of flavor, aroma and alcohol that creates your perfect Schnaps.

There are two parts to this chapter. First, I will describe the pieces of a still and how they are put together. That way you will know the equipment you will be working with. Then I will describe how to actually go about putting the mash into the still and drawing out the Schnaps.

COMPONENTS OF A STILL

Every still in the world, from Aristotle's desalinator to Jim Beam's biggest whisky machine, works on the same basic principles mentioned in Chapter 2. Two fluids with different boiling points have been mixed together. The still heats the mixed liquid to a temperature somewhere between those two boiling points. The liquid with the lower boiling point turns into steam and is collected into a separate container. Oversimplified, but essentially correct.

However, it is equally true that there are about a million possible variations of that process. All those different variations, and there are way too many to list here, have competing advantages and disadvantages for various kinds of drinks and distilling styles. This is another key area where a distiller's personal choices can make a big difference.

Schnaps falls right into that category. Different stills will make for different Schnaps. Not necessarily better or worse— just different. It depends on what the distiller is trying to accomplish. My goal here, however, is to give you the fundamental components of a still and the steps you will go through to distill your mash so that you can explore all of those variations on your own – once you have the basics down.

Every still has four primary components: (1) the pot, (2) the component on top of the pot (intentionally vague – see below), (3) the lyne arm, and (4) the condenser.

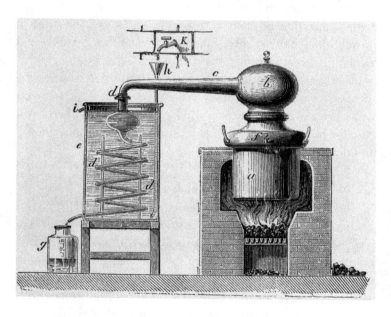

1873 Illustration of a Copper Still: Note the presence of all four basic parts.

The Pot

The pot is the large container at the base of the still. This is where the fruit mash goes when you are ready to distill it. The pot can be round, onion-shaped or maybe even conical. In larger, commercial-style stills, there is often a viewing glass on the side so that the distiller can keep an eye on the process.

The fundamental work of the pot is to heat the mash, and one of the major variations in pot design concerns how the contraption is heated. First, there are several different potential sources of heat. A distiller can use wood, steam, gas, peat or some other commercial source of heat to warm the mash. And some stills are constructed to let fumes from the heat source find their way into the distillate—think peat moss flavors in certain Scotch whiskies. So there can be a lot of variation in the heating source which can make a big difference.

The second heating question concerns how the heat is applied to the pot. The simple approach is for the heat to be applied directly to the bottom of the pot – like a cooking fire under a kettle. In most cases, this can work just fine for some very good Schnaps. The only thing to remember is that with direct heat, it is necessary to put a rummager at the bottom of the still.

A rummager is just a flat tray with holes (like a sieve) for the liquid part of the mash. The rummager's only job is to keep the solid part of the mash off of the bottom of the still. If that solid mash settles onto the bottom of the pot, it is very likely that the direct heat will burn or singe it. This will add a charred flavor to the distillate that you do not want. The rummager keeps that material off the bottom and prevents it from getting burned.

A direct heat still with a rummager can produce very good Schnaps, especially for the hobby distiller who is trying to keep costs down. However, there is a second option which typically only makes sense for larger operations. Most commercial distillers heat their stills with something called a double-jacketed water (or steam) bath.

In this type of heating set-up, the pot itself is surrounded by a bath of water or steam. The heat source itself is only directly applied to this outer bath where the water or steam is heated. That hot water or steam then transfers the heat to the pot itself. This is an indirect application of heat to the pot. Its primary advantages are that the pot is heated in a much more uniform manner and there is no direct application of the heat source to the pot or the mash in it. Consequently, the mash will not burn on the bottom and no rummager is needed.

The Component on Top of the Pot

The component, which sits directly on top of the still, is the piece of equipment which divides stills into their two primary categories—pot stills and rectifying stills.

In a pot still, this component is the swan neck. The swan neck can come in several different shapes and sizes, e.g. tall or short, straight or tapered. However, the swan neck does not really do much. Its primary job is just to funnel the vapor into the lyne arm.

In a rectifying still, on the other hand, the component on top of the pot is very important. It is called a rectifying column. The rectifying column is a long, vertical tube which connects the pot to the lyne arm at the top of the column. The rectifying column's job is to dramatically increase the alcohol content of the vapor. It does this by creating the equivalent of multiple distillations within a single run.

There are several different options for how the column does its job. In the most common version, the column is filled with some sort of small, particulate material like glass marbles or (clean and non-chemical) steel wool. The primary consideration here is using a fill material which has a lot of surface area.

The rectifying column causes the vapor to repeatedly condense and re-vaporize as it passes over the fill material on its way up the column. Every time some steam condenses and re-vaporizes, the distillation science is repeated, and the resulting vapor has a higher alcohol content, while the resulting water drips back down the column into the pot. Consequently, the final distillate that emerges from the still has a much higher alcohol content than a single run from a pot still.

Commercial Rectifying Column

This increased alcohol content from a single distilling run is the major advantage of the rectifying still over the pot still. To achieve the same high alcohol concentration with a pot still, the distiller may have to make multiple distilling runs with a single batch, once from the mash and then one or more times from the distillate. This increases the amount of time and effort it takes to produce a single batch of Schnaps. And it can be expensive for producing large quantities of Schnaps since heating sources do not run for free, and it may require more stills.

For a hobby distiller making typical Schnaps, it is almost certainly the case that a simple pot still with a swan neck will suffice. Depending on the alcohol content of particular mashes (given the type of fruit involved), it may still occasionally be necessary to make multiple runs with a pot still for a single batch.

A rectifying still is more expensive and takes more expertise to effectively operate, so a pot still with a swan neck is usually a good place for a hobby distiller to start. But if you ever decide to move into some sort of commercial production, you will probably want to look at rectifying stills.

The Lyne Arm

The lyne arm is a pretty straightforward component. It

connects the top of the swan neck or the rectifying column to the condenser. It is typically (though not always) tilted slightly downward and tapered toward the condenser. It funnels the vapor away from the heat so that it can be cooled and collected.

The Condenser

The condenser is typically a coiled pipe that descends from the lyne arm through a bath of cool or cold water. In this coil, the vapor condenses back into liquid due to the lower surrounding temperature. At the bottom of the bath, this new distillate flows out of the condenser tube into a waiting receptacle. Certain portions of this distillate need to be discarded, as will be discussed below, but essentially, this is the stuff you have been working so hard to produce. This is your concentrated ethyl alcohol, i.e. Schnaps!

Moonshine Still - Complete with all essential parts

THE DISTILLING PROCESS

Now you know the basic parts of the distilling apparatus. The next step is to figure out how to use it.

Conceptually, the next steps are easy. Fill the pot with mash and turn on the heat. Pretty soon, liquid will begin to drip out of the condenser. And there you go. Too bad it is not quite that simple. The challenge is that Schnaps is not the only thing coming out of the coil.

If you look back to the science in Chapter 2, you will recall that many different substances and types of alcohols can be and are produced in the fermentation process. Our goal is simply to maximize production of the one we want—ethanol—while minimizing the production of the ones we don't. Unfortunately, no matter how careful we are, every fermented mash will end up containing at least some small portions of the stuff we do not want.

Some of those unwanted substances, like acetaldehyde and methanol, have a boiling point lower than ethanol. This means they will vaporize sooner than the ethanol. Other substances, like fusel alcohols, have a boiling point higher than ethanol. This means that they will vaporize later than the ethanol.

It stands to reason, then, that the substances with the lower boiling points will come out of the condenser before the ethanol. This portion of the distillate is called the "head." We do not want to drink this. We will separate and discard it.

If we have a well-made mash, the next portion of the distillate (which should be by far the largest) is the ethanol. This is called the "heart" of the run. In our case, this is the Schnaps. This is the stuff we want to collect (and eventually drink).

The substances with the higher boiling points come out of the condenser last. They are known as the "tails." Again, we do not want to drink these. We will separate and discard them.

Obviously, the goal is to collect as much of the hearts as we can while avoiding the head and the tails as much as we can. It is also important to bear in mind that some of the substances in the heads are, in fact, poisonous, so it is important to address this issue with some care.

Determining the dividing lines between head, heart and tails is precisely where science meets art. There is no bright-line for dividing these portions, especially since they mix (at least a little) at both ends of the hearts run. And there may be some cases where a distiller finds that a small amount of the head or the tails actually enhances the flavor of the hearts. So here is another opportunity for a distiller to be unique.

METHANOL FACTS

In large quantities, methanol can irreversibly destroy optic nerves, i.e. cause blindness.

It is almost always present in all three of the heads, the heart, and the tails.

In small doses, it is harmless.

Dangerously high levels only occur in poorly-made liquors from dirty mashes.

However, there are a couple of rules of thumb which will help to find those invisible dividing lines. The first is temperature. The second is taste and aroma.

The temperature method involves regularly monitoring the temperature of the vapor at the top of the swan neck or rectifying column. In order to do this, the still must be equipped with a thermometer specifically designed for this purpose.

At the start of a distilling run, the mash can be rapidly heated. As it approaches boiling, however, the heating element should be moderated so that the mash does not boil too quickly. Given that the boiling point of the mash is somewhere between 78.5°C (173°F) and 100.0°C (212°F), the heat should probably be turned down somewhere between 60°C (140°F) and 70°C (158°F). A boil that is too hard and fast will result in too much mixing between the heads and the hearts because everything is heated up too quickly.

As the vapor begins to rise through the still head, make regular notes of the temperature. You will see it rise rapidly at first. Soon enough, the first liquid will start dripping out of the condenser. In virtually every case, this first fluid will be heads. However, the cleaner the fermentation process was, the shorter the heads run will be since most of these low-boiling point substances are a result of some sort of contamination of that process, i.e. rotting fruit, wild yeast, etc. (that is why it is so important to be clean and careful back at the fermentation stage!). Nonetheless, no matter how carefully the mash is fermented, there are almost certain to be some level of heads in any distilling run.

During this short run, continue to monitor the temperature of the steam which will still be rising relatively rapidly. The heads run is complete at the point where the steam temperature levels off and only continues to rise at a much more modest pace.

If you think about the science, this should make sense at this point. As the substances with lower boiling points (including ethanol) are boiled off, the boiling point of the remaining mash will rise (since more of the remaining liquid is water). So as the small amount of heads boils off, the boiling point of the remainder quickly approaches the boiling point of the ethanol/water mixture. But then there is a lot of ethanol to boil off (we hope), so the temperature sits at just about the same point while the ethanol is distilled. As that ethanol vaporizes, the boiling point of the remaining mash will slowly continue to creep up as the proportion of water continues to increase.

A similar process then takes place at the end of the hearts run. As the final ethanol vaporizes, the boiling point of the mash rises above the boiling point of ethanol and the substances in the tails begin to vaporize. However, there is less temperature space between the hearts run and the tails run since the mash is starting to approach the 100°C (212°F) mark (boiling point of water). Generally, once the temperature of the steam reaches 91°C (196°F), it is safe to assume that the distillate has now switched to tails.

For the distiller who likes more objective measures, this temperature method for dividing the distillate may work just fine. However, the whole point of Schnaps is the taste. So the more traditional method for dividing the distillate is by regularly sampling the taste and smell of the distillate as it comes out of the condenser. Obviously, this takes practice and experience.

To use this method, catch regular samples of the out-coming distillate in a teaspoon. To keep things simple, the heads will initially have a strong flavor and odor like cleaning solvents. To keep it even simpler, it will taste bad and not like Schnaps. Over the next several minutes, continue tasting the occasional sample. Over time, the distillate will begin to taste less like solvents and more like Schnaps. When the Schnaps flavor is sufficiently pronounced, switch receptacles. The fluid in the old receptacle is the heads. You can discard those. The nectar flowing into your new receptacle is the Schnaps.

The hearts continue for most of the run. But by regularly monitoring the taste, you will eventually notice that the Schnaps flavor will begin to fade, and other bitter flavors and aromas will begin to appear. This is the tails. As a general rule, switch to the tails sooner rather than later to avoid getting much of this in the Schnaps. Again, switch receptacles under the condenser. Typically, you will just discard the tails.

ALCOHOL STRENGTH

The only step left is to dilute your end product Schnaps to achieve your target alcohol content. It may seem counter-intuitive to *add* water to the Schnaps, which you just produced by *removing* the water. However, distilling obviously does more than simply remove water. It also pulls the alcohol and the flavor out of the mash so that you can put it in a bottle.

The alcohol content of drinking alcohols is typically expressed by ABV, i.e. "Alcohol By Volume." ABV refers to the percentage of the total volume of liquid which is actually ethanol. For example, 100 liters of 60% ABV alcohol contains 60 liters of ethanol mixed with 40 liters of water.

There is a lot of room for personal preference, but the ABV of a typical Schnaps is about 41-43%. At this level, the aroma and flavor of the distillate is maintained, but the burning sensation of the alcohol is reduced to a pleasant level.

The alcohol content of a good heads run is about 60-70% ABV. Consequently, it is typically necessary to add water to your distillate to dilute it down to a drinkable level. The alcohol content is usually measured with an instrument called a distilling hydrometer. The hydrometer is a long glass tube with calibrations along its side. It looks a lot like a very long, old-fashioned thermometer.

When the hydrometer is set into your distillate, the depth to which it sinks depends on the density of the fluid which is a function of the amount of alcohol present. The higher the alcohol content, the thinner the total mixture, and the deeper the hydrometer will sink. As long as the liquid is at the appropriate temperature (typically 20°C / 68°F, check the instructions on your hydrometer), the calibration on the side of the instrument right at the level of the liquid should tell you your ABV.

To reduce that initial ABV to the right drinkable level, you will need to calculate the correct amount of water to add. If numbers make you dizzy, and you plan to remain a hobby distiller, you can probably just estimate how much water you want to add, depending on what tastes good to you.

However, if you are trying to make a uniform product, or ever want to move into commercial production, you will need to get comfortable with a little funny math.

Consider this example. Assume that you have 70 liters of 65% ABV distillate, and you want to reduce it to a drinkable strength of 42% ABV. In your initial distillate, you have 45.5L of ethanol (0.65 x 70). Since you are only adding pure water, your final product will contain the same amount of alcohol but more water (hence the lower ABV). It would seem obvious that the simple equation for calculating how much water to add would look like this:

45.5 liters of alcohol ÷ X total liters of Schnaps = 0.42

This equation would tell you that you should add water until the total volume of your product is "X" liters. In this case, that would be 108.3 liters. Given that you started with 70 liters of distillate, you would just add 38.3 liters of water, and you would be all set. You would think.

It turns out that this equation is conceptually correct, but slightly wrong due to some pretty fascinating chemistry. When water is added to ethanol, the volume of the ethanol actually shrinks. The water and ethanol molecules mix in such a way that the total volume of the mixture is actually less than the sum of the original amounts. In other words, if you add 38.3 liters of water to 70 liters of an ethanol/water distillate, you will not end up with 108.3 liters of Schnaps. You will have slightly less than that.

In order to correctly calculate the right amount of water to produce a particular volume of Schnaps with a specific drinking strength, you will need to consult special tables which have been developed for precisely this purpose. The charts are built around liquids at particular temperatures, so you will need to make sure you follow their directions carefully, especially if you are aiming for uniformity among different runs. But once you get accustomed to the charts, it becomes a pretty straightforward matter to figure out the water to add.

And one last thought before you go start working on that funny math. Remember that the quality of the water you add is critical. Inadvertently using tap water with a high iron or sulfur content can completely mess up the flavor of your Schnaps and can cause it to get all cloudy, depending on the particulates in the water.

Your local tap water may be just fine. Or maybe your friend's tap water is cleaner than yours. Or you may need to buy chemical-free, distilled water at the store. Or you may have some other source of good water. Just be sure to check your water before you add it to your Schnaps. Do not let this final step ruin months of careful work.

~ CHAPTER FIVE ~

Schnaps without Distilling

So you would like to make your own Schnaps, but acquiring and operating your own still seems a little beyond your current ability or energy level. Not to worry. In this chapter, I will describe a method for creating a drink that can be a very passable imitation of good Schnaps, without resorting to a still.

Back in the introduction, I made reference to American-style schnapps. I pointed out that the low-quality stuff you usually get in the States is typically made by steeping fruit in stiff vodka for a couple of weeks and calling it schnapps.

Well, that is basically the technique I will describe in this chapter. However, the following pages will show you how to make a drink that is of generally good quality, and which I will still call Schnaps. And let's face it. Sometimes, a manageable Plan B is better than an impossible Plan A. By focusing on the quality of your ingredients, you can make a very good drink without doing your own distilling.

And this technique may actually provide a couple of advantages to the hobby Schnaps aficionado. First of all, it is easier. There is much less equipment involved. And it takes much less time and effort. Second, it avoids many (or most) of the legal restrictions which often surround Schnaps distilling. If your base alcohol (see below) is something you buy from a store, then you likely do not have to worry about any local laws restricting alcohol distillation.

On the other hand, there may also be a couple of disadvantages. First, there is something very satisfying about making your own Schnaps from beginning to end. You control the entire process, and you can claim the craftsman's ownership of your Schnaps. Second, your Beginner's Schnaps may not be a clear liquid, as most quality Schnaps are. Your Beginner's Schnaps will, in some cases, absorb the color of the fruit you are using. This does not really affect the taste. But it is a different outcome from distilling your own. So keep those advantages and disadvantages in mind as you decide which method of making Schnaps will work best for you.

Beginner's Schnaps is based on the fact that ethanol naturally draws out the flavor and the aroma of fruit steeping in it. You can use just about any type of fruit you want. In fact, this approach to making Schnaps actually allows for some experimentation beyond what is possible in a traditional process of fermentation and distillation. Given the fact that you do not have to worry about a successful fermentation, you can try fruits or other foods (like herbs) which might not otherwise have enough sugar to ferment. You can focus solely on finding flavors which might appeal to you.

The critical issue, and this should sound pretty familiar by now, is that the fruit is at its most ripe, is completely clean, and has had any damaged or rotting pieces removed. Any detritus or rot on the fruit will happily contribute its own flavor to your Schnaps if you let it.

Once you have determined the flavor element of your Schnaps, the next step is to choose the right alcohol to steep it in. This issue comes up because different types of fruit have different amounts of water in them. The water in the fruit will dilute the ABV of the original alcohol, potentially resulting in a weaker Schnaps.

This problem can be avoided with some forethought. If you

are making Schnaps from a fruit with a high water content, like most berries, for example, use a base alcohol with a higher ABV. The water in the berries will add to the total volume of the fluid in the jar, resulting in a lower total ABV.

On the other hand, if you are making Schnaps from a fruit with a lower water content – like apples – then use a base alcohol with a lower ABV. The smaller amount of water in the fruit will have less impact on the resulting ABV.

The following chart may give you some guidelines for what sort of alcohol may work with what sorts of fruit:

BASE ALCOHOL ABV	WATERY FRUITS
43%	Raspberries Cherries Watermelon
	NON-WATERY FRUITS
53%	Apples Orange peels Herbs

The ABV levels in the chart reflect alcohol concentrations you can usually buy pretty easily in most stores. But you should also bear in mind that there is plenty of room for experience and experimentation on this question. The ultimate goal will be to end up with a typical Schnaps ABV (41-43%), so you may want to err on the side of a higher ABV in your base alcohol, since you will likely need to dilute the final product in many cases anyway (see below).

The most likely candidate for your base alcohol is vodka. It has very little of its own flavor or aroma, so it will not compete with your fruit. You can also use a high ABV grain alcohol, which you intend to dilute substantially. The key is to make sure that the base alcohol does not have its own flavor which will interfere with the flavor and aroma of your fruit.

The final preparation step is to determine the container in

which you plan to make your Schnaps. A large glass jar is really the way to go. You should also be able to make it airtight. This will prevent any contamination during the steeping process.

Once you have selected your fruit and base alcohol, the process itself is relatively simple. Fill your jar about one-third full of your fruit. Then fill the remainder of the jar with alcohol. Then seal the jar. That's it.

Peach Beginner's Schnaps steeping

For best effect, the Schnaps should be allowed to steep for at least six to eight weeks. It should be stored at room temperature out of direct sunlight. Too much direct sunlight may cause the fruit in the jar (and the Schnaps) to turn an ugly brown color.

In most cases, it is no problem if the Schnaps is left to steep even longer. However, in the case of berries like raspberries or strawberries, they should not steep longer than eight weeks. Beyond that time, the alcohol will begin to absorb bitter flavors from the little seeds.

After the Schnaps has finished steeping, it is time to measure the ABV. Follow the instructions in Chapter Four to dilute your new Schnaps to the right drinkable level. When that is done, either drink the Schnaps immediately, or bottle it for enjoying later. In the bottling process, you may need to pour your Schnaps through a cheesecloth or other small filter to remove any floating particles.

A few recipes for Beginner's Schnaps which might help you get started follows.

APPLE SCHNAPS
- Start with about three medium-sized apples. Make sure to choose a variety with plenty of flavor and aroma. Cut each apple into about eight equal slices and remove the stems and seeds (including the tough pocket that surrounds the seeds.
- Fill a five-liter jar (with an airtight lid) about one-third full of the apple slices.
- Then fill the entire jar with 43% ABV alcohol (probably vodka) since apples do not have much water of their own.
- Seal the jar and set it in a dark, warm spot to steep for about four weeks. Shake it periodically to mix the apples through the alcohol.
- Give it a taste in about a month. If the flavor is full enough for you, then your Schnaps is done. If the flavor is too weak for you, then cut up some new apples and go through the process again (with the same alcohol).

HONEY SCHNAPS
This one is a little different since it does not use fruit. But as I said earlier, Beginner's Schnaps gives you a few additional options.

- For this recipe, begin with about two liters of 96% ABV alcohol next to the equivalent measure of water. (Notice that when you end up mixing the two fluids, you will end up with an alcohol content pretty close to typical Schnaps range.)
- Warm the water and stir in about two cups (500 g) of high-quality honey.
- Zest the peel of one lemon into the honey-water, and then pour the entire mixture into your five liter jar. Fill the rest of the jar with your base alcohol and seal the jar.
- Let the mixture steep until the fluid is entirely clear, and any detritus has settled to the bottom.
- Pour off the Schnaps and bottle it.

PEAR SCHNAPS

If you happen to live near a pear tree, there is a nifty "Schnaps" trick you can try in order to produce a very unique bottle of Beginner's Schnaps.[1] With some patience and fore-thought, you can produce a bottle of Schnaps, with a full-grown pear sitting on the bottom. When your friends see it, they will wonder how you got the fruit in there. Whether or not you tell them is entirely up to you.

- In the spring, after your pear tree has blossomed and the fruit is just starting to grow, find a couple of strong branches with young, small, healthy-looking pears at the ends.
- Slip a bottle with a slender mouth over each of the branches. Try to get the young pear as deep into the bottle as you can, to make sure that it does not ulti-mately grow in the neck of the bottle. And make sure the mouth of the bottle is pointed down, to avoid rain filling the bottle and ruining the fruit.

---

1   This trick will probably work for several different kinds of fruit. But pear Schnaps is one of the most popular Schnaps in the German-speaking world, and the "pear-in-the-bottle" trick is a common gift among Schnaps fans.

- Secure each bottle to its branch with wire or rope, making sure that the connection will survive typical wind and weather during the growing season. But also make sure that the wire or rope is not tied so tightly around the branch that it will kill the branch as it grows.
- Harvest the bottle, i.e. cut the branch, when the pear is ripe.
- Snap the pear off the branch, and remove any detritus from inside the bottle. Then carefully wash the pear (and the inside of the bottle) with warm water and a bottle brush.
- From there, proceed as normal. Fill the bottle with your

base alcohol. You will probably want to use 43% ABV alcohol so that you do not need to cut the Schnaps. This will prevent you from having to pour out and dilute your new pear Schnaps while the pear is still in the bottle. Then let the Schnaps steep. In this case, longer is probably better.

~ CHAPTER SIX ~

What the Austrians Call
Trinkkultur

So you have done all the hard work, and you have finally managed to make a great batch of Austrian Schnaps. The question now is—what do you do with it.

Sure, the simple answer is to tip it back and drink it down. Not a bad start at all. In fact, you should be sure to celebrate your success. But you probably made more than one or two glasses worth of drink. And after all that hard work, your Schnaps deserves a little special treatment. This chapter draws some ideas from Austria's *Trinkkultur* to get the most out of your Schnaps-drinking experience. What do we mean by *Trinkkultur*? It literally translates as "drinking culture," but it really refers to the whole spectrum of ways that alcohol is integrated into a deep and rich culture.

PRESENTATION

The first place to start is the bottle. You should store your Schnaps in clear glass bottles. That way, anyone who cares to notice will be able to see that you created a clean, clear Schnaps with no particles or pale colors (obviously excepting certain Be-

ginner's Schnaps!). A brown or green bottle will keep the Schnaps off of the floor, but it will hide some of the craft you put into the product.

And for sealing the bottles, there are two choices. The most traditional option is to use corks. That obviously requires a corker, and the corks are not re-usable. But they certainly make for great presentation. The second option is to use bottles that are made for screw-on caps. The caveat is that you must use metal screw-on caps—not plastic ones. The plastic in the caps and the alcohol in your Schnaps will not mix well.

Once you have picked out the bottle, the next place to give some thought to is the label. First, you definitely need to put some sort of label on your Schnaps. Once you have multiple types of Schnaps in your cellar, it can be easy to confuse them without labels since they are all clear. The easy route is to scribble the type of Schnaps onto a piece of masking tape and stick it on the bottle. But really, doesn't your artisan Schnaps deserve better?

A better way would be to produce your own well-designed, personal labels. There are many simple computer programs which will let you design labels on your own computer. And plenty of office supply stores can provide good quality labels. Put the two together in your printer, and you can come up with some very professional looking labels for your Schnaps.

From the bottle, the Schnaps next goes into your glass. The traditional way to serve artisan Schnaps is in a small tulip-shaped glass. This shape allows the aroma of the Schnaps to gather in the glass so that it rolls out into your nose when you take a sip.

A good aroma will add considerably to your enjoyment of the taste.

Lastly, good Schnaps should be served at about 18°C-20°C (65°F-68°F). Some places like to serve it really cold, but at that sort of temperature, very little of the aroma will come out. So let your Schnaps sit at room temperature for a few minutes before you pour it.

THE SCHNAPS CULTURE

So now you have a wonderful drink bottled and ready to be enjoyed. How and when you choose to drink it completes the story. This book will close with a few vignettes which demonstrate some of the wonderful ways Schnaps has enriched its native habitat in Germany and Austria. With any luck, these traditions will give you some ideas about how to make artisan Schnaps a colorful part of your own community and culture.

Verdauungsschnaps

The easiest introduction to the cultural side of Schnaps is a simple *Verdauungsschnaps*. This is a long, awkward German word, which just means a "digestive Schnaps." You may have heard the French word, digestif. It is the same thing.

A *Verdauungsschnaps* is just a glass of good Schnaps, which you enjoy after a meal. Its opposite is an aperitif, which is a drink before a meal. Interestingly, German keeps the French word for the pre-meal drink, but uses its own for the after-meal drink. Anyway, the aperitif is intended to stimulate the appetite. The goal of the *Verdauungsschnaps* is precisely the opposite, i.e. to calm the appetite.

Sharing a round of *Verdauungschnaps* with a group of family or friends around the table is one of the most satisfying ways you will ever find to finish a good meal.

St. Florian's Day

Saint Florian von Lorch is a Christian saint and martyr. He was born in the Roman city of Aelium Cetiumin (modern-day Sankt Pölten, Austria) in about 250 AD. He enlisted in the army and rose through the ranks until he was commander of the imperial army in the Roman province of Noricum (which is mostly modern-day Salzburg). One of his major responsibilities, in addition to his military duties, was organizing local firefighting brigades. Over time, he recruited and trained an elite group of soldiers whose sole duty was to fight fires.

During the widespread persecution of Christians by the Roman Emperor Diocletian in the early 300s, reports reached the emperor that Florian was not enforcing the persecution with sufficient vigor, so an investigation was launched. As part of the standard investigative procedure, Florian was ordered to offer a sacrifice to the Roman gods. He promptly refused to do so, revealing that he was, in fact, a Christian himself.

As punishment for the crime of being a Christian, he was sentenced to be burned at the stake. He is reputed to have told the Roman soldier about to light the pyre that, "If you do, I will climb to heaven on the flames." To avoid any potential celestial blowback, the Romans decided to drown him in a nearby river instead. The execution was duly carried out, and Florian died a martyr's death in about 304 AD. His body was later retrieved by the Christians in the area and interred at an Augustinian monastery near the city of Lorch.

Not surprisingly, St. Florian is today the patron saint of firefighters. Given the historic fear of fires in medieval and early modern Europe (most buildings were built of wood), he has played and continues to play an unusually large cultural role in many parts of Austria. The name Florian is virtually synonymous with firemen in the German-speaking world. A need for a fireman will sometimes be expressed simply as a call for Florian. And there are more than a few towns named after him.

St. Florian's feast day is May 4, and it is a pretty big deal in some places. St. Florian's Day, or *Florianitag* as it's called, typically begins with mass at the local Catholic Church. From there, the local village choir walks from house to house through town. At each house, the choir sings the local version of a well-known St. Florian song. There are many local variations of the song, but they are all some sort of request for protection over the house from fire.

After the choir finishes the song, the home's inhabitants come out and give the choir bread, eggs, lard, and, you guessed it—Schnaps!

Brass Band Competition

One of the most familiar features of German and Austrian culture is the well-known "oom-pah" band full of tubas and bass drums. Most towns or regions in Austria have their own local performance group. And these groups regularly meet together for festivals and other joint events.

Some of these festivals can include twenty or thirty different local groups of a hundred members per band. So they can be pretty big gatherings.

Obviously, each band is responsible for bringing its own instruments and uniforms. What might be less obvious is that each band also brings its own "refreshments." To be more specific, a band (consisting primarily, or exclusively, of men) often brings a "Schnaps girl" with them to their festivals.

The band members are all dressed in traditional Austrian outfits. And the Schnaps girl is no exception. She will definitely be wearing a traditional Austrian dirndl dress. And she may be carrying a small, wooden barrel on a strap slung over her shoulder. And what do you suppose is in that barrel? What else but Schnaps?

It can get pretty dry out there on the field playing your tuba. This might be the best solution imaginable. The Schnaps girl walks among the band members during their performances, providing a quick Schnaps wherever it might be needed.

Jauntaler Dreibergelauf

Austria's history and culture have deep roots in the Catholic Church. That is one reason why there are small chapels, statutes and other religious markers scattered throughout the mountains and along the trails of most of the country. One of the cultural habits that grew up along with those chapels and markers was a tradition of local pilgrimages to visit those memorials. One example of that tradition is the *Jauntaler Dreibergelauf*—the Jauntal Valley Three-Mountain Hike.

The *Dreibergelauf* happens every year around the beginning of May in the mountains of Carinthia, a province in southern Austria. And as you might guess, it traverses three local mountains (you probably guessed that). But the focus is really on the churches it visits.

The event begins with a midnight mass on a mountain in a small church called the Wallfahrtskirche am Lisnaberg, which, creatively enough, means the "Pilgrimage Church on the Lisna Mountain." From there, the pilgrims hike down through a small village called Aich, to another small chapel called the Church of St. Lucia. There, a deacon leads a prayer service.

After the service, the pilgrims take their first scheduled break. The locals traditionally provide them with fresh bread and warm tea outside the church.

After a rest, the pilgrims head for their next church, the Pilgrim Church of Heiligenstadt (and remember, it is just about sunrise at this point). Here they celebrate another mass. And then the local residents of Heiligenstadt show up with more food and coffee.

After this final scheduled break, the pilgrims hike back up the mountains to their last stop at the Pilgrimage Church of Heiligengrab. When they arrive, they are blessed with holy water by a local priest. They do a final lap around the church. Then they head into the church to meet up with other groups who have arrived from pilgrimages from other directions.

The *Dreibergelauf* is quite a hike. I suppose right now, you are asking what it has to do with Schnaps. Well, you have to remember that early May in the Alps is still pretty chilly, especially in the middle of the night. So what does one use to stay warm while hiking through the dark over the mountains? Schnaps, of course!

A regular feature of the hike is that some portion of the pilgrims will almost certainly have a couple of small bottles of Schnaps in their coat pockets to keep themselves and their fellow penitents warm. And nothing says 'religious experience' like a good bottle of homemade Schnaps.

Mandlberggut

This final passage has been appropriately reserved for one pocket of the world, which really exemplifies the "way of life" that was mentioned way back at the beginning of the book. I provide this information just so that you have one solid point of reference for Schnaps culture, as it can truly be understood.

In central Austria, near a little village called Mandling, there is a small farm and hostel up on the side of the valley. It sits at the junction of several footpaths which lead into the mountains rising up right behind the farm. The farm is called *Mandlberggut*.

It is certainly not a place most people will ever have a chance to visit. But the owners, the Warter family, understand and live the Schnaps way of life better than anyplace else I know.

Among numerous other activities, the Warters rent vacation space in a huge, old farmhouse next to their barn. They also operate a small restaurant where hungry hikers coming by can get something to eat.

But most importantly for our purposes, they also operate their own distillery. And one of their chief products is Schnaps. They sell their product right out of the distillery space. And upon request, Berhard Warter is happy to organize a Schnaps tasting for you and you friends, complete with a discussion about making Schnaps with the distilling master himself.

So if you ever find yourself sitting outside that huge farmhouse after a long day of hiking, surrounded by your family and friends, ask the Warters to pull out their little still and show you how they work their magic. That is the Schnaps way of life.

~ APPENDIX A ~

Schnaps and the Law

Distilling is a tightly controlled activity in a lot of countries. Particularly in the commercial context where liquor is produced for sale, governments make sure to get a big piece of the financial action. I am not really concerned with those commercial distillers here.

My concern here is with those of us who are interested in home distilling for personal consumption or as a hobby. In some countries, e.g. Italy, Russia, and the Ukraine, it is perfectly legal for individuals to manufacture distilled spirits for personal consumption. New Zealand became the newest of these enlightened countries to permit home distillation in 1996. But in many other countries with a strong distilling tradition, the laws can be quite a bit more complicated.

I want to make it crystal clear that I am not offering legal advice to anyone here. If you need the details, you need to contact an attorney. But the list below provides a summary of the legal environment for distilling Schnaps in the US and in the three countries with a strong Schnaps tradition.

UNITED STATES

I often hear people insist that they're "pretty sure" it's legal to distill small amounts of spirits in America without legal hassle, as long as it's for your own consumption.

Bad news, my fellow Americans. That sentiment is entirely wrong. Right now, it is illegal to make any amount of a distilled beverage in the US for human consumption without prior authorization of the federal government. Not a single drop.

This sad state of affairs has been true since Prohibition in the 1920s, and it is probably more about the tax revenue the feds suck out of small business owners than any sort of objection to distilling or drinking. Nonetheless, that is the law of the land right now in the US.

The federal agency which regulates distilled spirits, the Alcohol and Tobacco Tax and Trade Bureau (TTB), puts it this way in its online Distilled Spirits FAQs:[1]

> You may not produce spirits for beverage purposes without paying taxes and without prior approval of paperwork to operate a distilled spirits plant. [See 26 U.S.C. 5601 & 5602 for some of the criminal penalties.] There are numerous requirements that must be met that also make it impractical to produce spirits for personal or beverage use. Some of these requirements are paying special tax, filing an extensive application, filing a bond, providing adequate equipment to measure spirits, providing suitable tanks and pipelines, providing a separate building (other than a dwelling) and maintaining detailed records, and filing reports. All of these requirements are listed in 27 CFR Part 19. Spirits may be produced for non-beverage purposes for fuel use only without payment of tax, but you also must file an application, receive TTB's approval, and follow requirements, such as construction, use, records and reports.

---

1   Go to http://www.ttb.gov/spirits/faq.shtml#s7 for the original text

Clearly not for the faint of heart. Notice the references to criminal penalties among other things. Obtaining the requisite authorization to operate a still in America is not an easy task.

A similar prohibition used to exist for beer brewing in the US. However, in 1978, Congress passed a law which permitted Americans to home-brew beer in small batches for personal consumption. With a little luck, perhaps a similar exemption will one day be extended to aspiring distillers with a change in the law. But for right now, you cannot legally produce a single drop of liquor in the US without prior federal authorization.

GERMANY

Distilling in Germany is also pretty tightly-controlled, though the system there is not quite as restrictive as that in the US. There are two somewhat separate and parallel systems for monitoring and taxing liquor in Germany. Which of the systems controls a particular distiller depends on the type of distilling equipment the distiller uses.

The first system applies to *Verschlussbrennereien*. A *Verschlussbrennerei* is a still that has a particular piece of equipment attached to the end of the condenser, called a *Verschluss*, thus the name of the distillery. The *Verschluss* measures the amount and concentration of alcohol that comes out of the still. That amount and concentration determines the amount of tax due.

In theory, just about anyone can legally apply to operate a *Verschlussbrennerei*. There is not a limit on the number of licenses available for this type of still. However, the *Verschluss* is a pretty expensive piece of equipment, so it is generally only used by large, commercial distillers.

The system that generally applies to small distillers is for those who use a type of distillery called an *Abfindungsbrennerei*. This uses what we would usually think of as a typical still. There is no attached special piece of measuring equipment. Consequently, the distiller must manually report the amount and alcohol content of all mash that is going to be distilled. That way, the state can calculate the tax due.

The problem is that the number of *Abfindungsbrennereien* is limited by law to about 30,000. So for that reason, it is actually pretty difficult to start up a new still in Germany. The aspiring distiller has to wait for a license to be given up by someone else, which very rarely happens. In addition, an Abfindungsbrennerei is only allowed to produce a certain amount of alcohol every year. And further, every time a person buys a still, the seller is required to report the sale to the government.

The only loophole (and it is a small one) is for stills which have a pot holding less than 500 milliliters (that's 17 US fluid ounces – not much). Anyone is allowed to own and use one of those for home consumption. Basically, it is perfectly legal to have a little show-off still on the table. Beyond that, it can be pretty difficult to become a new, home-distiller in Germany.

Small, alembic still for home use

AUSTRIA

Austria has the same division as Germany between *Verschlussbrennereien* and *Abfindungsbrennereien*. In the case of *Verschlussbrennereien*, the situation is very similar to that in Germany. In theory, just about anyone may apply to operate such a still. However, given the expense, it effectively limited to commercial enterprises.

The law for *Abfindungsbrennereien* is a little different in a couple of interesting ways. In the first place, there is not a fixed number of distilling licenses available. So that is the good news. On the flip side, however, in order to qualify for a license, you must have your own source of fruit (or whatever you are using for mash). Typically, that means you have to own your own fruit trees or bushes.

And as in Germany, all stills must be registered with the government. Both the buyer and the seller are required to report a sale. The only exception here is for stills with a pot whose volume is two liters or less.

No later than five days before distilling, the government must be notified of the type and amount of mash to be distilled so that the proper tax can be calculated and paid. Naturally.

SWITZERLAND

The legal situation in Switzerland is a little different (which is often the case with respect to the Swiss). Switzerland has different categories for distillers than Germany or Austria. Big commercial enterprises which produce and market their own spirits are called *Gewerbebrenner*, or just commercial distillers. Note that nothing is said about what sort of technology is used to measure the alcohol (like a *Verschluss*). A second category of distillers is referred to as *Lohnbrenner*, or contract distillers. These are companies which distill products to-order for other parties.

The third category is the one which concerns us here. They are known as *Hausbrenner*, or home distillers—our favorite kind. In Switzerland, anyone can have a home still and produce

Schnaps for personal consumption as long as that person has his or her own source of mash, i.e. fruit trees or bushes. Further, all stills are required to be registered with the government. Most amazingly, Schnaps, or other spirits, can be produced for personal consumption with no tax paid.

~ APPENDIX B ~

German-English Glossary for All Things Schnaps

The Schnaps tradition comes from German-speaking central Europe, and many books and other materials about Schnaps are written in German. The following list of important German words about Schnaps may help you find useful information in some of those materials.

ABFINDUNGSBRENNEREI
One of the two primary legal categories for distilling in Germany and Austria. Tax due is based on the type and amount of mash which goes *into* the still.

ANGESETZTE / ANSATZ SCHNAPS
Beginner's Schnaps

APFELBRAND
Apple Schnaps

BRENNANLAGE
Still

BRENNEN

This verb literally means "to burn" or "to roast." However, it is the typical word most people use to talk about distilling.

BRENNEREI

Distillery

DESTILLIEREN

This is the more technical verb which means 'to distill.' Its meaning is clear, but it is not used nearly as much as 'brennen.'

GÄRSPUND

Airlock for sealing the fermenter

GÄREN

This verb means 'to ferment.'

GEISTROHR

Lyne arm. The word literally means 'spirits tube.'

GEMÜTLICHKEIT

Translates as 'coziness.' It is used to describe that happy state of affairs when you are among friends enjoying a good drink.

GEWERBEBRENNER

Commercial distiller: One of the three major legal categories of distillers in Switzerland. It generally refers to large, commercial enterprises.

HAUSBRENNER

Home distiller: One of the three major legal categories of distillers in Switzerland. It refers to hobbyists making spirits for home consumption from their own fruit or other mash.

HEFE

Yeast

KESSEL

Pot (as part of a still)

KIRSCHWASSER
Cherry Schnaps

KÜHLUNG
Condenser. The word literally means 'cooling' which makes a lot of sense.

LOHNBRENNER
Contract distiller:One of the three major legal categories of distillers in Switzerland.It refers to distillers who distill other people's mash in exchange for payment.

MAISCHE
Mash

MARILLENSCHNAPS
Apricot Schnaps

MITTELLAUF
The 'hearts' of a distilling run. The word means the 'middle run."

NACHLAUF
The 'tails" of a distilling run. The word literally means the 'after run.'

PROST! / PROSIT!
Cheers!

STEIGROHR
Swan neck. The word literally means 'ascending tube.'

TRINKKULTUR
Drinking culture. This word refers to the rich culture that surrounds good Schnaps (and other drinks).

VERDAUUNGSSCHNAPS
A Schnaps enjoyed after a meal to aid digestion.Equivalent to a *digestif.*

VERFLÜSSIGER
Literally 'liquifier.' It is the word used to refer to the pectinase added to mash to keep it fluid.

VERSCHLUSSBRENNEREI

One of the two primary legal categories for distilling in Germany and Austria. Tax due is based on the type and amount of distillate which comes *out of* the still.

VORLAUF

The 'heads' of a distilling run. The word literally means 'pre-run.'

ZUM WOHL!

To Your Health!

~ APPENDIX C ~

Additional Resources for the Aspiring Schnaps Distiller

ENGLISH-LANGUAGE RESOURCES

Germann, Thomas. *How to Start a Micro-Distillery for Under $50,000.* CreateSpace, 2013.

Gongery, Vincent R. *The Secrets of Building an Alcohol Producing Still.* David J. Gingery Publishing, 2012.

King, Jeff. *The Home Distiller's Workbook: Your Guide to Making Moonshine, Whisky, Vodka, Rum and So Much More.* CreateSpace, 2012.

Knoll, Aaron J. and David T. Smith. *The Craft of Gin.* White Mule Press, 2013.

Owens, Bill. *Modern Moonshine Techniques.* White Mule Press, 2009.

Owens, Bill and Alan Dikty, eds. *The Art of Distilling Whiskey and Other Spirits: An Enthusiast's Guide to the Artisan Distilling of Potent Potables.* Quarry Books, 2009.

Pischl, Josef. *Distilling Fruit Brandy.* Schiffer Publishing, 2012.

Rowley, Matthew B. *Moonshine!* Lark Crafts, 2007.

www.distilling.com: The website of the American Distilling Institute. If you are even remotely interested in craft distilling, this is the organization you need to know. It provides endless resources like conferences, trainings and publications. It is also where you will find many of your fellow craft distillers. It is the central gathering place for the entire craft distilling industry.

GERMAN-LANGUAGE RESOURCES

Herbst, Herbert. *Schnapsbrennen: Rezepte für Obstbrände und Ansatzschnäpse.* üdwest Verlag, 2004.

Malle, Bettina and Helge Schmickl. *Schnapsbrennen als Hobby.* Die Werkstatt, 2013.

www.mandlberggut.com: The website of the Warters' restaurant and hotel in central Austria.

www.schnapskultur.de: A fun website showing how Germans view their own *Trinkkultur*.